Biomes
of North
America

A Walk in the Prairie

by Rebecca L. Johnson

with illustrations by Phyllis V. Saroff

 CAROLRHODA BOOKS, INC./MINNEAPOLIS

For my niece Claire, who helps me see
the world with fresh eyes

–R. L. J.

Carolrhoda Books, Inc.
A division of Lerner Publishing Group
241 First Avenue North
Minneapolis, Minnesota 55401 U.S.A.

Website address: www.lernerbooks.com

Library of Congress Cataloging-in-Publication Data

Johnson, Rebecca L.
  A walk in the prairie / by Rebecca L. Johnson ; illustrations by
Phyllis V. Saroff.
    p.   cm. — (Biomes of North America)
  Includes index.
  Summary: Describes the climate, soil, seasons, plants, and animals
of the North American prairie and the ways in which the plants and
animals depend on each other and their environment to survive.
  ISBN 1-57505-153-2 (lib. bdg. : alk. paper)
1. Prairie ecology—Juvenile literature. 2. Prairies—Juvenile literature.
[1. Prairie ecology. 2. Prairies. 3. Ecology.] I. Saroff, Phyllis V., ill. II.
Title. III. Series: Johnson, Rebecca L. Biomes of North America.
QH541.5.P7 J65 2001
577.4'4—dc21   00-008252

Manufactured in the United States of America
2 3 4 5 6 7 – JR – 07 06 05 04 03 02

Words
to Know

BIOME (BYE-ohm)—a major community of living things that covers a large area, such as a grassland or a forest

CLIMATE (KLYE-mut)—a region's usual pattern of weather over a long period of time

GRASSLAND—a biome where the land is covered with grass and few trees grow

HIBERNATION (hy-bur-NAY-shun)—passing the winter in a special deep sleep

NECTAR—a sweet liquid produced by flowers. Nectar is used as food by animals such as bees, hummingbirds, and bats.

POLLEN (PAH-luhn)—fine, powdery material made by flowers. Pollen is usually yellow.

PRAIRIE—a type of North American grassland. Grasses and wildflowers grow well in the prairie, but it is too dry for most trees.

PREDATOR (PREH-duh-tur)—an animal that hunts and eats other animals

PREY (pray)—animals that are hunted and eaten by other animals

PUP—a baby prairie dog or coyote

SHORTGRASS—a type of prairie where little rain falls and grasses do not grow very tall

SOD—a dense layer of grass roots and dead grass that covers prairie soil

TALLGRASS—a type of prairie where enough rain falls for grasses to grow several feet tall

Tallgrass

swaying in the breeze

A mother prairie dog sits at the entrance to her burrow. Her pups play nearby. Tense and alert, she scans the low, grass-covered hills. Suddenly, a shadow appears on the grass. It glides toward the burrow. The prairie dog throws back her head and barks out a warning. *Yip-yip-yip!*

The pups come running as a red-tailed hawk descends. Its clawed feet are stretched toward them. The last pup dives down the burrow just in time. The hawk's claws close on nothing but air. It flies off to try its luck elsewhere on the prairie.

A prairie is a place of wide-open spaces. You can see for long distances.

Imagine an ocean where the waves are made of grass. That's what a prairie looks like. When the wind blows, the grass ripples like water. Here and there, a few trees and bushes grow along a stream or around a pond. But mostly there are just miles and miles of grass. It stretches out in all directions beneath a great dome of sky.

A prairie is a type of grassland. Prairie covers much of the middle of North America. It extends from the eastern side of the Rocky Mountains to Illinois, and from southern Canada to Texas.

Grasses like this Indian grass are the main plants on the prairie.

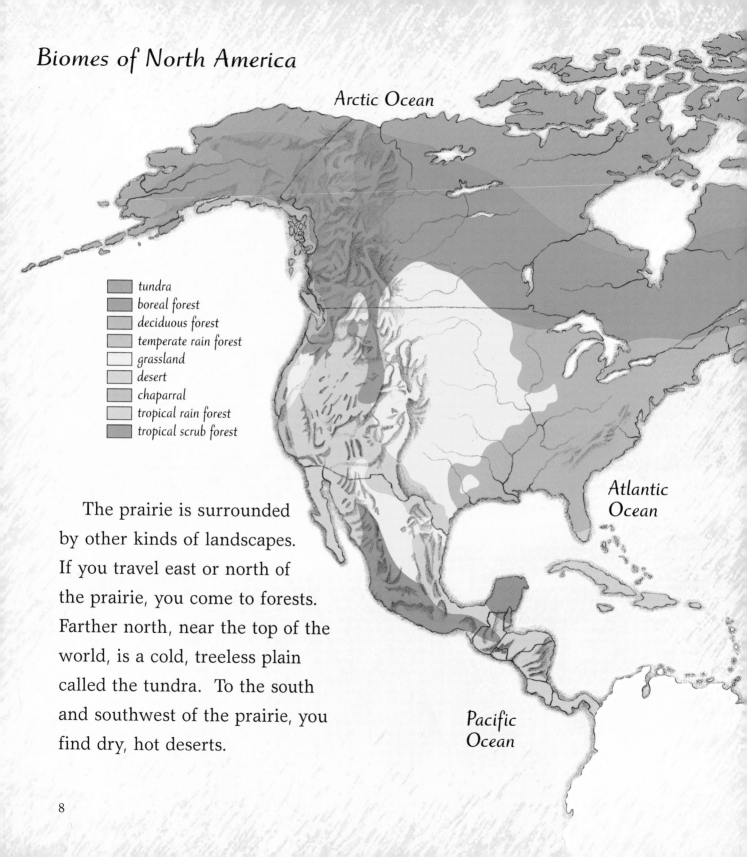

Biomes of North America

Arctic Ocean

Atlantic Ocean

Pacific Ocean

tundra
boreal forest
deciduous forest
temperate rain forest
grassland
desert
chaparral
tropical rain forest
tropical scrub forest

The prairie is surrounded
by other kinds of landscapes.
If you travel east or north of
the prairie, you come to forests.
Farther north, near the top of the
world, is a cold, treeless plain
called the tundra. To the south
and southwest of the prairie, you
find dry, hot deserts.

8

Grasslands, forests, tundra, and deserts are Earth's main land zones. Scientists call these different land zones biomes.

Each biome has a different type of climate. The climate is an area's usual pattern of weather over a long period of time.

Every biome is home to a special group of plants. The plants are well suited to living in that biome's climate and to growing in the soil found there.

Every biome is also home to a special group of animals. In one way or another, the animals depend on the plants to survive. Many of a biome's animals eat plants. Other animals eat the plant-eaters.

All sorts of wildflowers grow among the prairie's grasses.

9

All the plants and animals in a biome form a community. In that community, every living thing depends on other community members for its survival. A biome's climate, soil, plants, and animals are all connected this way.

The prairie's climate is quite dry—too dry for trees, but just right for grasses. Prairie winters are cold, and the summers are hot. The wind blows much of the time. Violent storms can spring up in minutes. Blizzards howl across the prairie in winter. Thunderstorms bring heavy rain, lightning, and hail—and sometimes tornadoes.

The wind blows most of the time on the prairie. Sometimes it's a breeze. Sometimes it's a howling gale.

Swirling winds create a tornado's funnel cloud.

A shortgrass prairie is found where the climate is dry and grasses don't grow very high (above). Big bluestem grass grows in the tallgrass prairie, where more rain falls (right).

If you traveled all the way across the prairie in the middle of North America, you'd discover that different kinds of grasses grow in different parts of this biome. In the east, where slightly more rain falls, you'd find grasses that are quite tall. Some kinds can grow taller than you! In the west, where it is drier, the grasses are shorter. Few grow more than knee-high.

Let's take a walk in the prairie. We'll see what life is like in this kingdom of grass and sky.

The tallest of all prairie grasses, big bluestem grows taller than most people do.

Grasses and other prairie plants use sunlight to make food (right). The plants are food for many animals, like this bison and her calf (below).

Every spring, warm winds blow up from the south. The winds and the sunshine melt the snow that has covered the prairie all winter long. As the ground thaws, narrow blades of grass push up through the damp soil. Soon the gently rolling landscape is covered in a bright green carpet of sweet-smelling grass.

Prairie grass isn't the kind that grows on a lawn It's wild. Dozens of kinds of wild grasses grow on the prairie. They have wonderful names like big bluestem, squirreltail, prairie dropseed, and devil's darning needle.

redtop

big bluestem

squirreltail

Dozens of kinds of wildflowers grow here, too. Prairie goldenpea, pale pasqueflowers, prairie violets, and pink shooting stars are some of the first to bloom each spring.

These delicate pasqueflowers grow only a few inches high (above left).

15

By midsummer, the grass is knee-high. Can you feel it swishing around your legs as you walk along? See how quickly the grass springs back up after you pass by?

Prairie grasses are tough, hardy plants. When the wind blows, their narrow green blades bend and sway—but they don't break. When you step on them, they straighten again. Hail may shred them. Animals may chew them to the ground. But before you know it, the grasses grow right back.

What is the grasses' survival secret? Blades of prairie grass grow up from strong roots. The roots spread wide and reach deep into the soil. Grass roots live for many years. No matter what happens to the green blades above, the roots usually survive—even when fire burns the grasses down to the ground.

Buffalo grass sends out low-growing stems called runners. Where the runners take root, a new plant grows.

A severe storm may pelt prairie grasses with icy lumps of hail, but the grasses' roots will remain alive underground.

17

Fires are common on the prairie. Most are started by lightning. Driven by the wind, a grass fire can race for miles across the prairie. It leaves nothing but charred, smoking ground in its path.

Within a few days, new shoots appear. Fires actually help keep a prairie healthy. They kill young trees and bushes that might shade the grasses or crowd them out. When the ashes of burned grass mix into the soil, they help new shoots grow quickly.

Fanned by the wind, a grass fire's flames leap high into the air.

Kneel down in the grass. Spread the blades apart, down to where they meet the ground. Covering the ground is sod—a layer of dead grass and the tangled roots of grass plants. Dig your fingers into the sod. Can you feel how dense and tough it is?

The tangled roots of prairie plants form a thick layer of sod on top of the soil.

Beneath the sod, the prairie soil is moist and dark. It is full of worms and tiny creatures that break dead grass and other wastes into smaller pieces. These pieces become part of the soil, which is rich in the things prairie plants need to grow well.

Tunneling earthworms help turn wastes into dark, rich soil.

All summer long, the colors of the prairie landscape change as different wildflowers come into bloom.

As you kneel here on the prairie, take a closer look at what's growing around you. Tucked in among the green grasses are all kinds of wildflowers. This time of year, the prairie looks like a crazy quilt of blossoms. Purple coneflowers and milkweed sway in the breeze. Delicate blue flax has petals the same color as the sky. The sweet smell of wild clover fills the air.

A wild rose plant
sprawls among
the grasses.

The flowers of black-eyed susan (above)
and purple coneflower (right) have
dark centers surrounded by bright petals.

23

Dressed in velvet colors, a butterfly lands on the flowers of an ironweed plant (above right).

Many of the grasses are blooming, too. Can you find their flowers? Most grow in clusters. The individual flowers are very, very small. It's hard to see them well without a magnifying glass.

All these flowers, large and small, attract bees, butterflies, and other insects. They visit the flowers in search of sweet nectar to drink. When insects land on flowers, yellow grains of pollen stick to their bodies. As insects go from flower to flower, they spread pollen from plant to plant. Plants use pollen to make seeds.

A busy bee collects
nectar and pollen as it
works its way around
a sunflower.

A monarch butterfly caterpillar crawls on plant stems in its search for food (above right).

Lie back among the prairie grasses and flowers. Watch the clouds float by, like giant cotton balls in the sky. Close your eyes and listen. Bees are buzzing. Crickets are chirping. And there's another sound—the faint munching of countless tiny mouths.

Prairie plants provide food for all sorts of animals. The most numerous grass-eaters are insects. Grasshoppers cling to green blades and stems. They gnaw them down to nothing, then leap away to the next meal. Caterpillars crawl along the edges of leaves, eating as they go. With strong jaws, beetles slice into anything green. Aphids suck juices from thick plant stems.

Field mice and voles nibble on prairie plants and feast on their seeds. So do ground squirrels, pocket gophers, and rabbits. They scurry along the paths they have made among the grass stems. They dig burrows in the soil, where they sleep and raise their babies.

A pocket gopher's front teeth grow through its lips. If it keeps its lips together, it can use those teeth to cut roots or dig without getting dirt in its mouth.

A ground squirrel stuffs its mouth with dry grass. It will use the grass to line its underground nest.

A killdeer pretends it has a broken wing to lure predators away from its eggs or chicks.

Bright yellow and black markings make meadowlarks easy to spot (above right).

Many kinds of birds live on the prairie. As you continue walking, a red-tailed hawk circles overhead. The loud, warbling song of a meadowlark rings through the air. A grasshopper sparrow lands on a thistle.

Some birds, like the hawk, live on the prairie year-round. Others spend only the summers here. They come to feast on insects and seeds, and to raise their chicks. The grasshopper sparrow is a summer visitor. It spends the winter in the south and flies north to the prairie each spring.

If you look carefully, you might spot the grasshopper sparrow's nest. It is on the ground nearby, a small cup woven of grass. Nestled in the bottom are four spotted eggs. Because there are few trees or bushes on the prairie, many birds build their nests on or just above the ground.

The eggs of a grasshopper sparrow lie safely hidden in a nest of woven grass (above). *A few days later, the sparrow is busy bringing food to its tiny chicks* (right).

When a rattlesnake bites, it injects poison through two long, hollow teeth called fangs.

Badgers eat ground squirrels and other small animals (above right). They use long claws to tear into underground burrows.

But the ground can be a dangerous place. There are many predators in the prairie. Badgers dig underground in search of prey. Bushy-tailed foxes wade silently through the grasses, sniffing for a meal.

Snakes also lurk in the tangle of stems and leaves. Snakes eat birds' eggs and chicks. They squeeze into burrows, looking for young mice or rabbits to devour. Most snakes, like bull snakes and garter snakes, are harmless to people. But rattlesnakes live here, too. So watch your step.

With dinner in its mouth, a coyote trots home to its pups (left). *A garter snake* (below left) *hunts worms, insects, and frogs.*

Coyotes are the largest predators in the prairie. They often stand very still in the grass. Only their ears move as they listen for the rustle of little feet or the squeak of a tiny voice. Then they pounce. Mice and rabbits are quick, but sometimes coyotes are quicker.

Prairie potholes become summer homes for ducks, geese, and many other birds.

Follow a gentle hillside down to a small pond. Tall reeds and cattails ring its banks. Shallow pools like this one are common in some parts of the prairie. Called "prairie potholes," they are nesting places for ducks and other summer birds. Both yellow-headed and red-winged blackbirds have built nests here. They perch on the cattails and shriek out rasping songs.

Red-winged blackbirds weave nests of soft grass near water.

A yellow-headed blackbird perches on cattails near the water's edge.

Prairie dogs often greet each other by touching noses, or "kissing."

Neat mounds of dirt mark the entrances to burrows in a prairie dog town *(above right)*.

Over the next hill, the land levels out. There isn't much grass here. The ground is covered with small mounds of dirt. Plump, squirrel-sized prairie dogs scamper among the mounds. You're standing on the edge of their "town."

34

Most of the town is underground. Prairie dogs live in burrows several feet beneath the surface. Sit quietly and watch them pop in and out of their burrows. Above the ground, some prairie dogs munch grasses. Others gather seeds. Some dig, kicking dirt high into the air as they repair old burrows or make new ones.

A prairie dog munches on grass (above left). Another uses its back feet to widen a burrow, sending dirt flying (left).

35

Slim, strong predators, black-footed ferrets hunt prairie dogs in their burrows at night.

When disturbed, burrowing owls make a noise like a rattlesnake to scare predators away.

Sometimes, other animals also live in a prairie dog town. A family of burrowing owls has made their home in an abandoned prairie dog burrow. Can you see their round, yellow eyes staring out at you?

All around the town, prairie dogs stand guard. They sit upright, with their paws folded neatly against their stomachs. They scan the landscape for signs of danger.

Yip-yip-yip! Something has alarmed the prairie dog guards. A herd of bison is coming toward the town.

Like a furry soldier, a prairie dog stands guard (left). A herd of bison moves slowly across the grassy landscape (below).

Bison are huge. The males, or bulls, are the largest and heaviest land animals in North America. Bison are well suited to life on the prairie. All they eat is grass. They can stand bitter cold, summer heat, and long periods without rain.

The bison are closer. Hear them snorting? Their heads bob up and down as they take big mouthfuls of grass.

A big male bison (right) *weighs as much as a small car. Bison calves have reddish fur that turns dark brown as they get older* (below).

A bison's horns are sturdy and sharp.

The prairie dogs dive into their burrows as the bison herd moves through their town. A few bison drop to their knees. They roll in the dirt, raising dust like clouds of smoke. These dust baths help keep biting flies away.

Bath time! A bison rolls in the dust (above left).

A pronghorn's large eyes are set on the sides of its head, giving it a wide-angle view of the prairie.

A young pronghorn follows its mother closely (above right).

The bison move on. Off in the distance, you spot a small herd of pronghorns. They move slowly, munching grass. There are several young pronghorns in the herd. They stay close by their mothers.

One pronghorn raises its head and sniffs the air. The whole herd is suddenly alert. A coyote leaps from a clump of thick grass. Instantly, the pronghorns are off and running like the wind.

Pronghorns are the fastest animals on the prairie—and in North America. Faster than racehorses, healthy pronghorns can easily outrun coyotes and any other prairie predator.

Kicking up their hooves, pronghorns bound across the prairie.

Autumn colors mean winter is on its way.

The prairie is full of wonderful sights and sounds at this time of year. But changes are coming. In a month or two, shorter days and cooler temperatures will mark the end of summer. Then flowers fade, and berries ripen. Seeds fall to the ground and are scattered by the wind.

When the first autumn frosts nip the air, the prairie changes from green to gold, then fades to brown. The grass blades turn dry as paper. Many birds take to the skies and head south.

By the end of summer, the center of a sunflower is packed with tasty seeds.

Ground squirrels grow fat from eating many seeds. Mice and prairie dogs fatten up, too. They also store seeds in their burrows for the long, cold months ahead.

As winter approaches, a thirteen-lined ground squirrel eats and eats and eats.

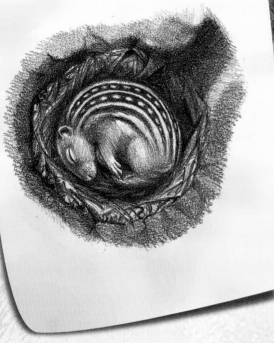

A bison pushes aside snow to reach the grass beneath it (above right).

One day in late October or early November, north winds bring snow to the prairie. The snow buries the dead grasses. It settles like a white blanket on the rolling hills.

The large animals brave many cold, snowy months. Foxes and coyotes hunt rabbits and mice. Bison use their huge heads to bulldoze away the snow. Then they can reach the dry but nourishing grasses beneath it.

Many smaller animals don't spend much time out in the snow and cold. They lie safe and snug underground, snoozing in their burrows. Some, like ground squirrels, fall into the deeper sleep of hibernation. Their body temperature falls to just above freezing. Their hearts beat slowly. They breathe very slowly, too.

In the rich, dark soil, roots and seeds survive, too. And so the animals and plants of the prairie pass the cold winter months, waiting for spring and for new life to return.

A dewdrop sparkles on a young blade of grass in the spring.

for further
Information
about the Prairie

Books

Berman, Ruth. *American Bison.* Minneapolis: Carolrhoda Books, 1992.

Gibson, Deborah Chase. *Foxes and Their Homes.* New York: Powerkids Press, 1999.

Kalbecken, Joan. *Badgers.* Danbury, CT: Children's Press, 1996.

Kops, Deborah. *Hawks.* Woodbridge, CT: Blackbirch Press, 2000.

Lepthien, Emilie U. *Squirrels.* Danbury, CT: Children's Press, 1992.

Patent, Dorothy Hinshaw. *Prairie Dogs.* New York: Clarion Books, 1999.

Staub, Frank. *America's Prairies.* Minneapolis: Carolrhoda Books, 1994.

Staub, Frank. *Prairie Dogs.* Minneapolis: Lerner Publications Company, 1998.

Winner, Cherie. *Coyotes.* Minneapolis: Carolrhoda Books, 1995.

Winner, Cherie. *The Sunflower Family.* Minneapolis: Carolrhoda Books, 1996.

Websites

Friends of the Prairie Learning Center
< http://www.tallgrass.org/ >

The website of the Neal Smith National Wildlife Refuge includes photos of the plants and animals that live there, as well as a kids' page with a prairie word game, nature hike ideas, and a kids' photo contest.

Highlands Middle School Prairie Project
< http://www.highlands.w-cook
.k12.il.us/Prairie/prairie1.html >

Sixth graders at this Illinois school researched the animals and plants of a local tallgrass prairie. Here you can read about their discoveries and take a virtual tour of the Wolf Road Prairie.

Underdogs: Prairie Dogs at Home
< http://www.nationalgeographic
.com/features/98/burrow/ >

The National Geographic Society
takes you underground into the
world of the prairie dog, where
you'll hear recordings of a prairie
dog's bark, chatter, and snarl.

What's It Like Where You Live?
Grasslands Page
< http://mbgnet.mobot.org/sets
/grasslnd/index.htm >

Read about the plant and animal life
of the North American prairie and
other grasslands all over the world.
You can also take a virtual tour of a
prairie in summertime.

Photo Acknowledgments

The photographs in this book are
reproduced courtesy of: Len Rue, Jr./©
Leonard Rue Enterprises, pp. 4–5; © Tom
Bean, pp. 6, 10–11, 12–13, 13 (bottom) 14
(both), 16, 20, 32–33, 37 (both), 41, 45; ©
Richard Day/Daybreak Imagery, pp. 7, 9,
18–19, 22, 25, 29 (both), 33 (bottom), 42; ©
Kent and Donna Dannen, pp. 15, 23 (all), 38
(both), 43; © Layne Kennedy/CORBIS, p. 17;
© Dwight Kuhn, p. 21; © Gary Braasch
Photography, pp. 24, 26; © John Gerlach/
Visuals Unlimited, p. 27; © Wendy Shattil/
Bob Rozinski, pp. 28, 36, 44; Daniel J.
Cox/naturalexposures.com, pp. 30, 35 (both),
40; © Ed Degginger, p. 31 (top); © Bill
Beatty/Visuals Unlimited, p. 31 (bottom); ©
A. Benton/Visuals Unlimited, p. 34–35; ©
Wm. Grenfell/Visuals Unlimited, p. 39.

Front cover photographs by: © Tom Bean
(background, foreground); © Kent and
Donna Dannen (middle).

Index

Numbers in **bold** refer to photos and drawings.

DATE DUE
